Rainbo`

Book of Poetry

Lily Lawson

THE
WRIGHT HOUSE

Rainbow's Yellow Book of Poetry is the third book in the Rainbow series.

Yellow is for me a happy colour. It means sunshine and positivity.

It has been said I have a positive world view.

I believe there is more 'good' than 'bad' in the world and there is 'good' in all humans, even the ones we label 'bad'.

To me it is important to label actions rather than people and to attempt to understand before we criticise. We don't always get it right. We're human. We can but try.

I hope the poems I have included in *Yellow* raise a smile and bring you happiness.

Help me share that stuff around. We need as much as we can get in this world of ours.

Happy reading.

Contents

Today

In the early morning,
possibilities seem endless,
the day stretching ahead,
hours yet to fill,
demands we must address,
the joy of sweet surprise
may visit us today.

Perhaps the phone will ring,
a message will raise a smile,
the sun will glisten or
rain will help the flowers grow,
we will hear a favourite song,
we will remember
to be thankful.

Talk to me

Something's written on my forehead
That maybe you can see.
My reflection tells me nothing.
It's invisible to me.

I know exactly what it says.
It's clear as it can be.
At least it is to others.
It just says 'talk to me.'

Everybody does it.
I wish not to complain.
When I think about it,
it does sort of explain.

When I'm in a restaurant,
in a shop or at the match,
on the bus or at the station,
at a show I hope to catch.

While I'm waiting in a queue
or walking down the street,
the words become quite visible
to everyone I meet.

I've met all kinds of people
and learnt all sorts of stuff.
I wouldn't be without it
even when the going's tough.

I have had it all my life
as far as I recall.
It's there, so if you need it
it's always free to all.

That thing called love

I love you.
Simple words
that mask the complexity of relationship.
Yet my heart knows
that this feeling inside me
we label love
is a simple thing,
despite its many outfits
and aliases,
and its constant reinvention.
You are ever changing.
As am I.

But this thing that grows
within us
that we can't imagine life without,
that lives almost as a separate entity
even if it survives on crumbs.
If it were ripped away
would wound in ways
that could not heal.

Yet knowing that
we took the risk.
It's worth riches beyond measure
to truly, purely, love another
and have that love returned.

Unbreakable

It did not break
when it was tested.
It took an unexpected shape
remaining intact,
worn threads preserved
with tender care.

It lost its newness,
that joy recalled in memory
bringing a smile,
spurred to cherish
the tattered thing
that held them fast.

Despite the trials,
the bits reduced,
almost transparent,
a single strand
in place of once strong rope,
it did not break.

Undefeated

It did not go away.
I shooed it,
threw whatever was to hand.
It remained defiant.

I removed my attention,
it ignored me back
but still
it did not go away.

I shouted,
sang, jumped, and danced
laughed so long and hard it hurt.
It turned away

I turned out the light.
The coldness of evening came.
In the morning it was there
it did not go away.

I left the door ajar.
The days of unmovable existence
emitting from it
made me brave.

It crept in unseen.
In the living room it waited
victorious and smiling.
It did not go away.

The Chair of Life

Life is a chair in which we sit.
We are at birth allotted it.
Some can be adjusted so
our legs can be both high and low.
We move it to adjust the view
to see if we find something new.
We add cushions and some throws
and don't let folks make off with those.
From time to time, it fits quite well.
Sometimes it's lumpy bumpy hell.
It can at times require a mend
or comfort us like it's a friend.
If we treat it with much care
we might enjoy just sitting there.

It might be for the best

It might be for the best they say,
whoever 'they' may be.
It can be hard to determine
what the best might be.

Life isn't always this or that
and even when that's so
complicated situations
can leave us struggling to know.

If we take a left turn,
would we wish we had gone right?
If we choose to walk away
would it have been wise to fight?

There are no easy answers.
It can feel like a test.
If we meet the unexpected
it might be for the best.

The boxer's commute

I bob and weave around human
obstructions.
Legs and spirit grow weary with each round.
Rules constructed for those who fail to
follow.
No referees' whistle out here in the wild.

There is no corner to rest between my
battles.
My water must be wrestled from my bag.
The sweat that drips, absorbs into my
clothing.
The gloves are off as we go charging for the
doors.

Senses of life assault me from all angles.
The pole I hold escapes my line of vision.
I tense my arm to stay upon my feet.
My travel kit is clamped between my legs.

Focusing my gaze towards the nearest
window.
Each pause in transit requires a body shift.
The crowd thins out, each part of it
defeated.
Glory refuels me as I leave the ring.

Choices

They exchanged that glance that mingles
hope and fear.
Which this was decidedly unclear.
The incessant beating of their racing hearts.
The unexpected could tear their world
apart.

A moment that might alter fate
stood waiting for them at the gate.
To embrace it or to walk away?
A decision must be made today.

Hiding

We bury ourselves in stuff.
it's selection and acquisition a distraction.
Cocooned in barriers of possessions.

When we shift and sort
we emerge as who we truly are
and expose that self to the world.

What's important

It's the togetherness not the where that
matters.
It's whose voice you hear when the silence
shatters.
It's the way you end the thoughts
unfinished.
The love you share that won't be
diminished.
An act, a word in haste forgiven.
If to love all your thoughts are driven.
The whole is bigger than the sum of its two
parts
when those two things are two people's
hearts.

Rain

The rain fell on the dappled hills
and ran in rivers down the mountainside.
I will gladly go back there again
to have you touch me
like you did in the rain.

Hope

In the senselessness of this situation
I cling to hope.
The companion that sleeps with me,
eats with me, drinks with me,
sits next to me in silence
while I empty my soul.

As the words pour from my fingers
I realise that hope is on the page
in the uninterruptible scrawl of ink,
tangled in my words,
securely attached, visible.

Hope has entered my heart,
set up home within me.
It refuses to leave.

Recipe for Care

Take a bowl of kindness.
Add a portion of love,
mix with care.
Bake daily on medium heat.
Divide as meets the needs of the hungry.
Accept offerings in return
with grace
regardless of
quantity,
quality,
frequency,
or hunger.
Do not take more than you need.
Share if necessary.
Be prepared to go without on occasion.
Feed yourself in times of rationing or
famine
and others as you are able.

My favourite things

I love the ever-changing sky,
blues and greys giving way to pinks,
oranges, reds and black,
the stars and moon a glimpse into the
vastness of the galaxy.

I love the wind in my hair
gently ruffling, like a favourite aunty's hand
showing affection,
or using its strength to rearrange it in
unnamed styles.

I love the rain,
it equalises, freedom, isolation, space,
as people are driven from streets or are lost
in their fight against it.

I love the sun
warming my skin, delicate touches, teasing
or covering my whole body until I'm driven
to seek cover.

I love the sound of waves crashing on the
beach,
tidal rhythm, powerful, noisy, gently edging,
covering all in their path, marking their
territory.

I love the sight and sound of a river
finding its way as it travels over rocks,
powerful, welcoming, mesmerising.

I love to hear children playing,
uncontained excitement, screeching,
laughing, singing, talking to each other.

I love eating chips outside,
picking them up with my fingers, saltiness
attaching to my skin,
the air adding to the atmospheric
experience.

I love warm doughnuts
straight from the basket, covered in sugar,
warmth spreading through my body each
time my teeth sink in.

I love the smell of a swimming pool
its unique aroma, alluring, calling to me,
familiarity, knowledge of expected calmness.

I love the smile on a child's face,
genuine, innocent, free, a moment of joy
expressed without hesitation or reserve.

I love the sight and smell of a candle,
solid shape, changing almost unnoticeably
flames extinguished; the aroma remains.

I love the smell of baking bread,
tempting, drawing me in, a reminder of
deliciousness,
resistance is futile, warm packages begging
to be devoured.

I love mulled wine
the spirit of Christmas caresses my mouth,
touching every taste bud, carrying love
through my veins.

I love looking at photographs
memories captured, posed, or shot in the
moment
part of life's story, half-forgotten yesterdays.

I love a roaring coal fire
filling the room with warmth like a hug,
it's fascinating method of destruction,
twisting, charring, melting.

I love the taste of orange juice,
the freshness running down my throat,
wakening my enthusiasm for the day.

I love the smell of peppermint tea,
soothing, working its magic before the first
sip,
the daily ritual bringing me peace.

I love chocolate,
biting it before it disintegrates in my mouth,
leaving a sliver of taste on my tongue when
it dissolves.

I love listening to my favourite music,
history mingles with the present in jukebox
style shuffle,
rock, pop, country, big band, easy listening,
theme tunes ...

I love a hot shower,
cleansing water pouring over my skin,
warming me from the outside in.

I love to hear the voice of a friend,
via telephone, on video, or face to face,
speech communicates a quality inaccessible
by text.

I love a hug,
arms wrapped around in an expression of
love,
holding on, unsure when to let go.

They're not like you

They can talk
but not like you.
They can answer my questions,
make me laugh,
remind me of days gone by,
pull me out of my head,
motivate me,
encourage and praise me,
chastise me when I'm bent on causing
trouble,
lift me up,
make me smile,
correct my misinformation,
educate me,
help me deal with my mistakes,
hug me,
listen,
tell me stories,
make me a better person.
Do almost everything that you do
but not like you.

Somehow

I just knew.
Don't ask me how,
I just did.

It was like some invisible thread
connected us,
pulling us together.

I was instantly captivated.
The spell has not worn off,
I'm grateful to say.

The original sparkle dulled a little.
Removing the outer layer
revealed something more beautiful.

What we have
is unexpected,
more precious than gold.

I am allowed feelings

My feelings are valid.
They need no seal of approval.
They don't need editing.
They are not mislabelled.
They are tiny and lost
in a collection outnumbering the football
crowd.
They are huge and unavoidable.
They swagger around
demanding attention.
They are beautiful.
They are ugly.
They are real.
They are mine.

Okay without you

I expected to miss you,
to yearn for your words,
your absent wisdom
to leave me wanting
abandoned, lost,
searching for replacement.
Uniqueness is irreplaceable.

The days following your departure
filled with strangeness
expectation of a brief appearance
hard to overcome,
but I settled in
to life without you.
You are not dead.

I cannot bring myself to hate.
Strength of feeling stops short,
indifference takes its place.
I no longer want or need you.
What I thought we had is
lost forever. There is no us.
I am fine, I am enough.

Remember Me

Maybe one day
you will have walked away
moved on without me,
left whatever this is far behind.

But you will see something
inhale a fragrance,
or hear some music,
you will think of me,
who we used to be,
and smile.

Baggage

Black night diminishes.
The speck of light we anticipated grows.
The uniqueness of each day
reflected in the music of its beginning.

Surrender
Relief
Joy
Hope,

emotional spaghetti twisting us.

Yesterday,
today,
tomorrow,

a tangled heap.

Things we shed along the way

picked up,
examined,
given back,

the lightened load heavier again.

We find a home for all we cannot carry,
recognise it had something left to teach us,
but hadn't found the right time to let it go.

There is no sunrise without singing.

Mournful,
calm,
joyous.

It's up to us to find our song.

After Lockdown

The sun crept through the fog
revealing a glimpse of the world long
unseen.
During it's time beneath the fog
changes had occurred in the world.
The humans had learned many things
including which others they found valuable.
They had learnt to adapt to the fog
finding ways of addressing their needs
without journeying too far into it.
Realising the simple things of life
were worth more than they knew
they carried them as they journeyed
into the brave new world.

Moving on

The chapters of our lives
bring forth change,
adjustments to our way of living.
Characters arrive, depart,
play a stronger or lesser role.
It makes us pause
considering how to edit ourselves
what to take forward
what to leave behind.

The power of words

They are but words.
Yet we are writers.
We know their power.
Letters arranged in ways
to convey meaning.

Words making sentences
paragraphs, pages,
chapters, books.

From our lips,
from our pens and fingers
we share, we make people think,
feel, connect.

We support and oppose.
We speak truth and lies.
We hide. We baffle and confuse.
We explain, accept, deny.

If our words inform,
inspire, incite,
does that bring pride?
Fear? Safety?

Do we just talk?
Or can we listen?
Can we debate?
Can we change the world?

Standing on the shoulders of giants

Words from poets gone before
who pushed at or kicked in the door
demanding and expecting more
than what they knew to be the score

Creating and abandoning rhyme
warriors of space and time
voicing thoughts inside their heads
filling folks with fear and dread
was that really what they said?

In written or in spoken word
knew how to make their voices heard
that make a reader crave a book
squirreled in a reading nook

I thank each and every one
the ones still living and those gone
to mangle words of yesterday
it looks like poetry's here to stay.

Now you've read my book

don't forget to review
Amazon, Goodreads,
Bookbub too!
Thank you very much
I'm counting on you!

Lily x

Acknowledgements

Thank you for reading my book.

Thanks to Ann Garcia for the cover.

Thanks to Cheryl whose red marks I work to eliminate.

To Jo and Dreena whose poetic knowledge exceeds mine.

To Cin, Fi, and Carolyn.

To my J's, my Wordy's, the Write Clubbers, the Dream Team and TTAB.

To Christine and Anita.

To Butterfly who makes my world more yellow than she knows.

To every poet published or otherwise whose poetry has found its way to me or is yet to make the journey.

Thank you for your words.

By The Author

Poetry Books

My Fathers Daughter,
A Taste of What's to Come,
Rainbow's Red Book of Poetry
Rainbow's Orange Book of Poetry
Rainbow's Yellow Book of Poetry

Short Stories

Sandcastles

Kids' Books

Santa's Early Christmas,
The Palm Tree Swingers Island Band
If I Were Invisible…

Lily's Amazon

Rainbow's Red Book of Poetry

'Do yourself a favour: buy this, curl up in your favourite chair and read it, knowing you will come away refreshed.'

Life is a complex thing. As social beings, we live side by side, sometimes in not so harmonious circumstances. This book celebrates love and tackling the challenges we face as humans. Control is not always ours.

Keep learning.
Keep growing.
Be yourself.
Do your best.

Life is complicated, yet very simple.

'These poems are layered and more formal -- with an air of William Blake or even Christina Rosetti -- but without pretension or anachronism. They still have the Lawson touch.'

'Lily Lawson has this way of making me weep.

And dance.

And understand myself a little better.

And understand others, perhaps, a little better too.'

Rainbow's Orange Book of Poetry

Lily Lawson's poems work on a deep level in my heart. She weaves a tiny story out of exact chosen words that strike at my core.
Get a cup of tea or coffee, sit back, and savor her poems. Your day will be better for it.

Orange means passion, and for Lily Lawson, that's writing. In this second relatable, contemporary collection of the Rainbow series, the 'non poetry-lovers poet' shares that passion in the way only she can.

'... to the artist, the poet, the dreamer,
the weaver of words,
I give thanks.'

'However the reader interprets the intent in these poems, they are all written with Lily's usual word craft, and emotion without sentiment.'

'... full of poems that are simple and sincere, heartfelt but without the veil of unnecessary complexity that often obfuscates rather than illuminates, and that puts many readers off.'

' ... this slenderest of volumes will appeal to the writer in all of us.

About the Author

Lily Lawson is a poet and fiction writer
living in the UK.
She has poetry, short stories,
and creative non-fiction
published in anthologies and online
in addition to her books

You can find out more about Lily
and read more of her work on her blog.

You can follow her on Amazon
where you will find her books.

Printed in Great Britain
by Amazon

47902014R10046